# A Little Bit of Me

# A Little Bit of Me

## Carol Anne Skipper

# CONTENTS

# Carol Goes Shopping

*Well, here I am a little bit bored*
*and thinking what to do*
*I know, I'm quite good with words,*
*I'll write a poem for you.*

*So here we go, it would be fun,*
*I hope you will agree,*
*Tell me how you are coping,*
*add a verse, or two or three.*

*I went to Aldi, got there at eight*
*and joined the back of the queue*
*When I got inside there was nothing left,*
*Oh dear, what shall I do?*

*Off to Sainsbury's, oh joy of joys,*
*I got potatoes and wine,*
*some shampoo and a toothbrush*
*and tomatoes on the vine.*

*Then to Lidl, much the same,*
*all the shelves were bare*
*No bread, no milk, no dog food,*
*I really do despair.*

*So, Tesco was my next stop.*
*Yippee!! A litre of gin,*
*some tonic and some lemons*
*and baked beans in a tin.*

*So next it's into Morrisons,*
*Oh, things are looking up!*
*I got some whisky and cheddar cheese*
*and two dozen 'soup in a cup'!*

*It's beginning to get dark now,*
*I've one last shop to go*
*My final trip is to Waitrose,*
*for posh people don't you know.*

*I've got 2 lobsters and champagne*
*and pâté de foie gras*
*I'm homeward bound and very tired*
*just need petrol for my car.*

The Next Day...

*I've just been to the Co-op,*
*t'was not much left within*
*I bought 6 doughnuts, a sausage roll,*
*and another litre of gin.*

*Next port of call was Poundland,*
*Oh, what a lovely place,*
*I went berserk, I'm afraid to say,*
*new make-up for my face.*

*I got some coloured pencils,*
*I can't admit defeat,*
*I've purchased all this rubbish,*
*but I've nothing yet to eat.*

*I got some varnish and false nails,*
*felt tips and a colouring book,*
*A pink princess tiara,*
*to complete my trendy new look.*

*There's no point in going shopping,*
*all the shelves are bare*
*Some people's greed and selfishness*
*leaves you pulling out your hair!*

Carol Anne Skipper

On 23$^{rd}$ March 2020, Boris Johnson told the country that we were in lockdown. To stop the spread of Covid 19 we had to stay indoors, only coming out to shop for food or exercise.

# It's All Gone Wrong

My waxed jacket is leaking
Tiles blown off the roof
I'm putting on a few pounds,
Jeans tight so that is proof.

The toilet it is block-ed
Drain rods I need to find
Water gushes from the hot rail
Floor needs mopping, what a bind.

The rain is never ending
The gutters overflow
When will things start to go right?
The answer – we don't know.

Zumba and Pilates
Are our saving grace
We chat and laugh, and exercise
On Zoom in our own little space.

*I look into the kitchen*
*Jack and Lulu snuggled there*
*Time for tea and biscuits*
*In my big soft comfy chair.*

*Perhaps life isn't so bad*
*Not all doom and gloom and sorrow*
*So, I'll do the housework next week*
*And start my diet tomorrow.*

*One day I will be famous*
*And make a lot of money*
*But until then I will make you smile*
*I hope my poems you find funny.*

*PS... My washing machine is broken*
*The socks they didn't spin*
*There is only one solution*
*I'm opening that bottle of gin...*

*5/1/21*

# I Will Go Down to the Sea Again

(With sincere apologies to John Masefield)

*I will go down to the sea again*
*To the lonely sea and the sky*
*I thought I'd go to Eastbourne*
*Or Norman's Bay nearby*
*And the long walk in the sunshine*
*And the warm water breaking*
*And a blue sky on a perfect day*
*And a blue sea baking.*

*I will go down to the sea again*
*For the call of the running tide*
*Perhaps I'll go to Dover*
*But no ferries will be spied*
*And all I ask is a normal day*
*With the "stay at home" lifted*
*And the cure found and the hours long*
*And the nurses committed.*

*I will go down to the sea again*
*To the vagrant gypsy life*
*To the good times and the old times*
*With freedom and company rife*
*And all I ask, when the end's in sight*
*For our NHS superheroes*
*Give them decent pay and rewards deserved*
*When the death toll zeros.*

7/4/20

# You Know
# Who You Are

*Looking out of the window, I wonder what became,*
*Of boyfriends long departed, I still remember their name.*

*The first one was called Alan,*
*he had red hair and spots,*
*But his kisses made my hair curl,*
*I loved him lots and lots.*

*The next was Phillip Juniper,*
*Yes, I remember him well,*
*With hair like Mungo Gerry,*
*big sideboards, and a nice smell.*

*He was such fun to be with,*
*and he had a happy face,*
*Also, an Austin A30,*
*we went all over the place,*

Carol Anne Skipper

*We visited Shepton Mallet,*
*a pop festival no less,*
*We swam at Frensham Ponds,*
*in a state of much undress!!!*

*We rode upon his motorbike,*
*to a blues club in Godalming,*
*Drank Newcastle Brown from bottles,*
*before it was the done thing!!!!*

*Then I moved to Oxfordshire,*
*and Jill arranged a blind date,*
*I thought John very handsome,*
*we fell in love; yes it was fate,*

*We were together a year or so,*
*our feelings deep and true,*
*When he asked, "Will you marry me?"*
*I said, "Yes I'll marry you,"*

*I knew at the reception*
*I'd made a big mistake,*
*But what could I do, but carry on,*
*happiness was easy to fake!*

*He wasn't the man I had loved*
*he was jealous and violent and cruel,*
*I suffered, believing he would change,*
*I stayed for 2 years; what a fool!.*

*Tony phoned to ask me out,*
*I said, "I don't know who you are,"*
*"Make yourself known to me please,*
*next time you hire a car."*

*He had a slow and purposeful walk,*
*as befits an officer of the law,*
*He was kind, a proper gentleman,*
*and one I began to adore.*

*We went to a famous country club,*
*in elegant clothes I looked super*
*We drank champagne, we dined and danced*
*and laughed with Tommy Cooper.*

*I remember spending a whole weekend*
*in very close proximity,*
*Something I had not done before,*
*or since, with anybody!*

*Then he moved from town to country,*
*I was sad, our love at its end,*
*I think I cried for about a week,*
*but then my heart did mend.*

*I was called as a witness to a North London court,*
*Unfortunately, I had lost my voice,*
*I told the police, I couldn't go,*
*but they said I had no choice.*

*So, alone I stood, waiting to be called,*
*when Garry spotted me,*
*He took me down into the cells*
*and bought me a cup of tea.*

*I left the court without farewell,*
*but he followed me into the street,*
*He said later he knew I was special,*
*and on Saturday we planned to meet.*

*His brother was very famous,*
*wish he'd hinted what the stars foretold.*
*We moved in together, had our future planned,*
*with Hatton Garden emerald, set in band of gold.*

*But he was omnipresent,*
*he ran my bath and meals prepared,*
*He worried if I was a few minutes late,*
*He destroyed the life we shared,*

*So, I called the whole thing off,*
*and he took back the ring!!!!*
*I was a bit annoyed by that,*
*it was such a beautiful thing.*

*Tim had just been promoted to sergeant,*
*moved to a new station that day,*
*He asked a PC to show him their patch,*
*and pretty girls along the way,*

*So, they drove to the car hire company,*
*where I was hard at work,*
*My staff made them tea and flirted,*
*not best pleased, I said, "Girls don't shirk."*

*A few months later a dance was arranged, by me,*
*to say, "Well done, thank you girls.",*
*The local police were told of the date,*
*there he was, sparkling eyes, dark brown curls.*

*But my darling it was not to be,*
*wrong place, wrong time, neither totally free,*
*We both had constraints, and so we did part,*
*But the memory of you is still deep in my heart.*

*Oh, my dearest Tim,*
*so many years have passed and yet I say,*
*My broken heart and my love for you*
*has not faded away.*

*He was undercover, flared jeans,*
*long hair, no hat,*
*But kind face, and a warm smile,*
*we'd talk about this and that.*

*He came in fairly often,*
*if he thought his "cover blown,"*
*He'd phone and say, "Can I change the car?"*
*Seeds of affection gradually sown.*

*One day he said, "Won't be in for a while,*
*I'm off to Tenerife."*
*I sarcastically said, "Send a postcard",*
*Spanish holidays were beyond my belief.*

*The postcard arrived and upon his return,*
*In the pub he bought every round!!!*
*He gave me a warm happy feeling,*
*a new boyfriend I had found....*

*He didn't ask me out again,*
*and I did wonder why?*
*His friend Bob stood behind him,*
*and whispered, "Because he's shy,"*

*He said, "I've a camel's bladder lamp*
*at my third floor flat in Chelsea."*
*I thought, "I bet he's married,*
*I'd better go and see."*

*That Christmas he gave me some jewellery,*
*The box said it came from Bond Street,*
*I loved that silver bracelet, and thought,*
*I've really landed on my feet!*

*Now Elizabeth Duke (of Bond Street) is Argos,*
*I found out to my dismay!*
*But it didn't really matter,*
*I wore it anyway,*

Carol Anne Skipper

*We met in 1975 and we are still together today,*
*He's solid, honest and reliable, one upon whom I depend,*
*He loves me and looks after me,*
*no matter what life may send.*

*So, there we are, what's been has gone,*
*And time like a river flows forever on*
*Chances missed, memories kept, happy times and sad ones too,*
*So, with such deep affection, I remember every one of you!!*

*24/11/20*

# Desperate For Company

I thought I'd hold a séance, I need some company,
No one would know they came here, only the dogs and me,
So, I cut out letters A to Z, and two saying YES and NO,
The numbers 1 to 10 were next, and on the table, they did go,

I placed a wine glass upside down, a most unusual sight!
I took deep breath, with curtains drawn
Eyes closed, candles alight.
Well, I waited for a feeling, a knock, a movement, a sign,
I asked, "Is anybody there?" Slight tingle down my spine,

My arm is starting to ache, I rest my elbow on the table,
I ask again, "Is anyone there, send me a sign if you are able."
I alter my touch on the glass, my right arm is causing me pain,
Wait, is that a tapping on the window?
No, just a splatter of rain!

My bottom is going numb; I should have sat on a cushion,
I'll have to use my other arm; I get up and change my position,

*Now I need to regain concentration;*
*I'm bored, losing the will to live,*
*And perhaps, in the current circumstances,*
*not a phrase that I should give.*

*"Give me a sign" I whisper, and the curtains blow inwards,*
*away from the windowsill,*
*But that's just what happens with badly fitting windows,*
*and you live on top of a hill!*
*My eyes open wide, but there is no one there, no manifestations,*
*no knocks, no sign,*
*So, I take the glass from the table, go into the kitchen*
*and fill it with wine!!!*

*19/2/21*

# Home Together

We received an e-mail last weekend,
Addressed to my husband, not me,
It came from the NHS and said,
He was now "High Category,"

On 16th February he had a special birthday,
One ending in a nought,
It started with a seven,
Neither of us gave it much thought.

But suddenly he had to shield,
He'd worked through lockdowns three,
They said he'd have to stay at home,
They didn't consult me!

Perhaps I don't want him here each day,
At work is where he should be,
He'll get in the way, disrupt my routine,
He'll make too much mess, I like it tidy,

*But I had no say in the matter,*
*Sent home from work the next day,*
*I kindly gave him the afternoon off,*
*And asleep on the settee he lay.*

*He returned home with treats and a smile,*
*2 Greggs sausage rolls for my lunch,*
*He's bought plants for the garden,*
*He's up to something, female intuition, a hunch,*

*On Tuesday, up, showered and dressed by 8.30,*
*I have instigated many house rules,*
*The radio it can play softly,*
*But no back-to-back Only Fools,*

*He popped into work Tuesday morning,*
*He had to send off certain forms,*
*Then he said he'd go shopping,*
*Wear his mask, thus avoiding all germs.*

*Well now we have several packets of crisps,*
*Two pizzas and a steak and ale pie,*
*A current loaf, white wine, and beer,*
*What happened to healthy eating? I sigh.*

*Well Wednesday didn't go to well,*
*It's 9.30, he's in bed asleep,*
*I've finished my Pilates class,*
*And find it hard my temper to keep.*

*By Thursday suddenly my man has changed,*
*he's done a lot of jobs about the house,*
*The back door is mended, the summer house stained.*
*I'm a very happy, loving spouse.*

*But now he's Mr Grumpy,*
*in the car, shopping, I went for a ride,*
*The day was hot; I put the window down,*
*IT STUCK! now upwards it will not slide,*

*Good God, you'd think the world had ended,*
*He will not talk, coffee left, gone cold in his cup,*
*He's taken the inside of the door to bits*
*He is cold and very cross, still the window won't go up*

*So now he's gone into "Over Sulk",*
*into the bedroom, asleep on the bed,*
*Do I ask him what he'd like for dinner?*
*Or find a wall on which to bang my head?*

Carol Anne Skipper

*Well, what a difference a day makes!*
*He phoned our mechanic called Ken,*
*Who explained, wedge it up with some wood,*
*bring it down to the garage, next Monday at ten.*

*The rest of the day went quite well,*
*now he's cooking chicken and veg stir fry,*
*I'm knocking back white wine, eating crisps,*
*with feet up, on settee I lie.*

*It is still going better than planned,*
*with new handle on the kitchen door,*
*These minor imperfections that constantly irritated me,*
*have never bothered him before.*

*Two years ago, we began to lay a shingle path,*
*all around my yellow and white garden shed,*
*It would have a "Seaside Theme"*
*be the special "Me" place I wanted.*

*35 bags of shingle laid so far,*
*another 40 should about do it,*
*Then I will have my special retreat,*
*and in shabby chic, rocking chair sit.*

*In fact, I must secretly admit; it is quite nice having him here,*
*I now know why I love him; he really is a dear,*
*And possibly he's enjoying not working full time,*
*And possibly he's enjoying being with me,*
*And possibly he'll decide to retire,*
*I'll just have to wait and see!!!*

*12/3/21*

# My Friend Sue

My friend Sue has joined a dating group,
She seeks male company,
Just someone to make her laugh
And take her out to tea,

She wants someone to chat to
And pass the time each day.
Hopefully, mutual interests,
Could affection come her way?

Now Sue has got a few in tow,
She chats on the internet,
There is one in France, of whom she is fond,
Due to Covid they haven't met,

Others seem too good to be true,
They are handsome, articulate and funny,
Oh Sue, we all implore you, please,
Please, don't lend them any money.

*There is one called Anthony, near Arundel,*
*With rugged good looks, who speaks French,*
*He was a pilot, RAF, now retired,*
*Or possibly a con, a massive pretence,*

*Another called Richard an ex-MEP,*
*Again, too good to be true,*
*Her intuition tells her he's married,*
*And she is not sure what to do,*

*They first met in Oxted, a pleasant afternoon*
*Sitting outside they had cups of tea,*
*He made her laugh, they got on well,*
*And conversation flowed easily,*

*They have met a few times since,*
*He advised and helped her prune fruit trees,*
*He's been to her farm, assisted with lambs,*
*Stayed for lunch, she felt very at ease,*

*But, unless she e-mails him,*
*And, unless she instigates their next "date",*
*There is no contact from him,*
*And this attitude is beginning to grate,*

*So, will they meet again?*
*Well, here is the thing,*
*He said he is separated, not divorced,*
*But he still wore his wedding ring!*

*There are so many more,*
*Of whom I will recite*
*But I will give you a precis,*
*Or we will be up all night.*

*Duncan owns a Scottish Isle,*
*Ex-Army PT instructor and outward bound,*
*Striking a pose, in his skimpy speedos*
*T 'would make many a girl's heart pound.*

*So why is this hunk all alone?*
*Something doesn't ring true, and rather arrogantly,*
*He states "If distance is an object,*
*Then you are not the girl for me."*

*Next Gordon from Cranbrook aged 54 (and the rest)*
*He played piano and ukulele,*
*But with beard, moustache and monocle,*
*He wasn't the one for Susie*

*Now Alan, a teacher from Kent,*
*Who was overweight, and unable to spell,*
*Then Allen from Cambridge, no photo supplied,*
*Who had shingles and was very unwell.*

*Then there was Kevin, blue eyes and bald,*
*From somewhere up int' North West,*
*He kept snakes in his back bedroom,*
*And a spider tattoo covered his chest.*

*It is rather sad that people of a certain age,*
*Are alone and in need of a companion,*
*But my dear Sue is loving it,*
*Still searching for her D'Artagnan!!*

12/3/21

# The Sea

Just blue sky, warm air and me
I love the sea,
Just Jack for company,
I love the sea,
Just the sun on my body,
I love the sea.
Just surrounded by beauty,
I love the sea.

On isolated beach
No one in sight
Sea to ankles reach,
Waves to knee height,

Idyllic solitude,
Sand soft beneath toe,
Footprints don't protrude,
Waters constant flow.

*Tide moves silently,*
*Covers all before,*
*Never violently*
*Creeping towards shore,*

*Miniscule crabs,*
*Rock pool clear,*
*lift rock slabs,*
*Translucent fish appear.*

*Anemone's tentacles,*
*Explore and retract,*
*Collect Blue Mussels,*
*Edible seaweed hacked.*

*Tide now at its height*
*Calm sea sparkling,*
*Dolphins jump with delight,*
*Sun's rays cooling.*

*Daylight fades to dark,*
*Sun on horizon low,*
*Distant Basking Shark,*
*Lighthouse sweeping glow.*

*New moons ark,*
*Stars appear above,*
*Now hidden by dark,*
*The sea that I love.*

13/3/21

# Winter Sunrise

Far to the east the day begins,
With light, but pale and low,
Then, within seconds, a tender hint of rouge,
On the horizon show.
The promise of colour becomes a dot,
Increasing bit by bit,
Until what was so small, rises higher,
And the sky is gently lit.

Crimson tentacles creep and claw upward
and outward, across the sky,
All colours of molten shade,
Jostle and push together and lie,
Dark yellow shows beneath the reds,
Shining out, add grey and blue,
Indigo and violet levitate and merge,
In ever changing hue.

Carol Anne Skipper

*All colours spread, escape, converge,*
*Light comes from below,*
*Ever changing tapestry, reflecting through clouds,*
*Orange ball with warming glow,*
*Beams from sun pierce through sky,*
*Colours seep and wane,*
*Ever floating higher*
*She casts light on her domain.*

*1/2/21*

# Still In Lockdown

My hair is looking messy
Growing longer every day
Lowlights, Highlights disappeared
And my roots are turning grey.

I haven't put on make-up
For over 4 weeks now
We will be 'staying at home' until
Politicians do allow.

I am unable to meet friends
To eat and laugh and chat
I'm getting better with technology
Well, I should be grateful for that.

I've sorted out the cupboard
Beneath the bathroom sink
There's pills and potions, creams and gels
And 12 hand soaps coloured pink.

*There is stuff I got for Christmas*
*And stuff I bought myself*
*There is stuff I'll never ever use*
*So, I remove it from the shelf.*

*My little car is very sad*
*He's not been out for ages*
*With spider's web on the steering wheel*
*And dust on all his gauges.*

*His little bonnet is no longer blue*
*His windows dark with grime*
*One of his tyres deflated*
*I'll wash him, I've got time.*

*A nest of dormice beneath the seat*
*They really are so cute*
*I cannot leave them in the car*
*They are re-homed in an old welly boot.*

*I hide them very carefully*
*Deep in the barn of hay*
*I hope they stay safe and grow*
*And eventually move away.*

May 2020

# Remembrance

*They will not see tomorrow*
*Or remember yesterday*
*At eleven we stand erect and proud*
*Whilst in silence we remember and pray.*

*There will be no fancy wedding*
*No newborn's hand to hold*
*No grandchildren to play with*
*As you will not grow old.*

*You will not be forgotten*
*You did not die in vain*
*But honoured and respected*
*By those that still remain.*

*And yet they haven't left us*
*Who died so gallantly*
*Their spirit will continue*
*Live on in you and me.*

2019

# Snow On a Sunday Morning

The grass, once green, now white and
pitted with sharp overnight frost,
Troubled grey clouds, brooding, all is still.
Sinking slowly sky descends onto trees
Which stand upright and defiant on top of the hill.

With merest whisper, a snowflake falls,
And others follow, yet make no sound
In eerie light, with no word spoken
Thick layer of snow covers the ground.

Large bushes, once upright and proud
Bend and collapse with sudden weight,
A robin hops and chirps with glee
As fragile little feet touch rotten gate.

Carol Anne Skipper

*Many fields distant, a tiny house*
*Shrouded in mist, roof camouflaged under snow,*
*Barely visible, yet you know it there,*
*Two windows, like amber eyes, aglow.*

*Black lines between the fields,*
*Hedges not quite engulfed by snow.*
*Grey horses appear, then disappear,*
*Only fading hoof prints indicate where they go.*

*The flakes of snow now hurry down*
*And swirl and twist in dizzy dance,*
*Just stand, enjoy, breathe deeply in*
*And let this beauty your life enhance.*

24/1/21

# Bye Bye Donald

I'm sitting here all alone
And feeling a little bit blue
I used to have a good job
Now I've got nothing to do.

I've pardoned all my cronies,
They are out of prison and free,
So, whatever favour I desire
They will always be in debt to me!!

I've disposed with most on death row
Innocent or guilty, doesn't bother me!
So, commit fraud, or tax evade
For me it's normality.

So, America put it to the vote
I won 'easy' another 4 years
"But what" an anomaly, "It's fake"
I shout and dissolve into tears.

*"I did win, I did, I did"*
*Won't have it another way*
*Ok, so no proof or evidence,*
*CNN, BBC, fake news every day.*

*I'll search and search and find them,*
*Those thousands of missing votes,*
*They shoved us out the back door,*
*No time to get our coats.*

*But I showed them what I'm made of*
*No one gets the better of me,*
*I took out all the light bulbs,*
*And the paper from each lavatory!!!!*

26/1/21

# Another Lockdown Day!

Oh, this rain will it never stop?
Continuous sound plip plop, plip plop.
Whilst up int'north it is deep snow,
How long do we wait for the sun to show?

The wind is fierce, the ground is soggy,
Can't ride my horse or walk my doggy.
I've done all the housework, need something to do,
I'll mend that chair, with superglue.

I'll watch a film and have some tea,
I'll phone up Sally, need company.
Dye my hair, yet again, hide grey roots,
I'll sort out clothes, throw away old boots.

I'll sit and watch the rain and mist,
I've tons to do, I'll write a list.
Can't do washing, it will not dry,
I search the larder and find fruit pie.

*I decide to save it for later on.*
*Phone rings, automated voice, a con?*
*The rain continues pouring down*
*Green face mask on, keep still, don't frown.*

*I've plucked and shaved nearly all my bits,*
*Tummy getting fat, T-shirt only just fits.*
*So, do not, in the mirror look*
*Put the radio on and read your new book.*

*I've painted that wall with coral red*
*Before you know it will be time for bed.*
*Well, my day has gone quite fast, had no time for sorrow,*
*The only problem I can see, is what to do tomorrow.*

*Well, here we are the following day,*
*It's now gone nine and in bed I lay.*
*Just what is there to get up for?*
*I reach out, pull yesterday's clothes from the floor.*

*Day after day, same old, same old*
*Make an effort, out of bed I rolled.*
*I drink my tea and look out at the rain,*
*Oh well, it's just yesterday all over again.*

3/2/21

# Jo Sally in Devon

I'm fed up doing housework,
I'm fed up dying my hair
It always goes too dark
When I choose a shade that's fair.
I go into the bathroom; I have a little wee
Then go into the kitchen and make a cup of tea.

I'm fed up with the cold and wet,
I'm fed up now it's snow,
I wander aimlessly around my house
Picking up things as I go.
I go into the bathroom; I have a little wee
Then go into the kitchen and make a cup of tea.

I re-arrange the cushions,
Place the curtains in folds neat,
I straighten the pictures and water the plants
The tour of my house now complete.

Carol Anne Skipper

*I go into the bathroom; I have a little wee*
*Then go into the kitchen and make a cup of tea.*

*I look for something I can paint*
*Or something I can mend,*
*I turn the lights on, then off, then on again,*
*I'm going slowly round the bend.*
*I go into the bathroom; I have a little wee*
*Then go into the kitchen and make a cup of tea.*

*8/2/21*

# In Memory of
# Captain Sir Tom Moore

*When you walk through a storm hold your head up high*
*Has there ever been a more inspiring song?*
*To give Determination, Hope, Courage, not tears,*
*Sing, take comfort, be resilient and strong.*

*Outside is bleak, inside we are alone.*
*Each day is the same as the last,*
*Imprisoned in our homes, nothing to do or say*
*There seems no future, no past.*

*But how long do we have to wait?*
*Look towards the golden sky*
*We must be positive, believe,*
*Just walk on, walk on, and I'll tell you why.*

*Two angels watching over me*
*They surround me with aura gold*

*I often feel their presence*
*As my body, in their power, they hold.*

*They give me hope, we are not alone*
*Someone loves you and will keep you safe*
*Keep going, tomorrow will be a good day,*
*So, with hope in your heart, have faith.*

*8/2/21*

# *Desolate*

*One special person I deeply loved*
*Has gone, too late to say goodbye*
*And yet I can be with him again*
*He's in my dreams, when in bed I lie.*

*My anguish is a physical pain*
*My emotions so raw I can't describe*
*My sadness so deep, so desolate*
*I don't know how I'll ever survive.*

*But keep going I will, I must,*
*No one comprehends my broken heart laid bare*
*Except my most trusted female friends*
*With whom, my ultimate secret, I share.*

*I walk, I don't see my surroundings*
*I breath, can you hear my pain?*
*I cry, do you feel my sadness?*
*Unable to speak, tears fall like rain.*

*Did you just go to bed, never to awake?*
*Or sit in the chair and feel unwell?*
*The truth I will never know*
*And you are unable to tell.*

*You were alone when you left us*
*As I am alone now, but muddling through,*
*I gaze up at the stars, scattered across the sky*
*And remembering our love, I wonder which one is you.*

February 2021

Addendum

*Can you see me? Are you with me?*
*Will you keep me safe each day?*
*There is no grave to visit*
*Nowhere to lay flowers and pray,*
*Nowhere I can open up my heart*
*And tell you as I've written here.*
*Nothing can change the past*
*Not even love so deep and sincere.*
*And when I get the final call*
*And knowing you are waiting near*
*At peace I will rise upwards*
*And let go gently without fear.*

February 2021

# First Covid Jab

The e-mail arrived on Wednesday,
We were watching The Street on TV,
Invited to attend for a Covid jab
Asking when would I be free?

Husband replied in minutes
Thursday pm or Friday would do
Back came their reply, so efficient!
Giving day, date, time, in marquee new.

I said, "I'm not sure where to go"
He said "Do not get upset,
I'll take the morning off work,
I'll drive you, no need to fret".

Appointment confirmed in Crawley, this week
We arrived just before ten,
We sat in reception, I filled in the form,
Hubby returned to the car, me next then.

*Jenny was very chatty, put me at my ease,*
*Warm, kind with years of dedication*
*"Roll up your sleeve", she gently said,*
*"And I'll do your vaccination".*

*God, that really hurt*
*I jumped, huge intake of breath*
*"Relax, relax" she kept saying,*
*"It's for your own good and your health".*

*Well finally the pain stopped*
*And the needle from my arm withdrew,*
*Into the third waiting area,*
*But no biscuits, or warming brew!*

*I waited 10 minutes and they let me leave,*
*I'd had no serious reaction*
*We shopped for a few unnecessary bits, but then*
*I felt very cold and tired, wobbly, too weak for interaction.*

*I felt that I'd been beaten up*
*Done 10 rounds with Muhammed Ali*
*My head thumped, my bones ached*
*What was happening in my little body?*

*I had no appetite*
*My mouth of cardboard tasted,*
*I shivered and I shook and cried*
*Hid under heavy blankets, totally wasted.*

*I only felt very slightly better,*
*It was Sunday evening I think,*
*I ate a warming Sunday dinner*
*And a few brandies I did sink.*

*Well now I can only sit and wait,*
*Till my second vaccination is due*
*On 30th April at 10am,*
*I'll let you know how I do.*

12/2/21

# The End of an Affair

Lots of things left unsaid
A jumble of words inside my head
Lots of tears left to fall
Knowing you despise it all
Many dreams to fulfil
And yet, I wonder if we will?
Many days of laughter and love,
Caring and sharing, special secrets we have.
Too much doubt is seeded by pain
Empathy, trust, hard to regain.
Too many nights spent all alone,
Wondering where your future has gone.
Many paths and travel sore,
A crossroads where we've been before,
Many memories cannot fade, and yet
Given time we will forget.
Lots of reasons our love can't die
We must savour, not supress, or say goodbye,
Lots of words, all with meanings,
Especially 'I love you' whispered with feelings.

1994

# How To Write a Poem

It's not hard to write a poem
If you do not try, you'll never know
What you could achieve from your heart,
Paint with words, let them mingle, melt and grow.

The first line can rhyme with the third,
The second line rhyme with the fourth,
Perhaps tell of your favourite bird,
Recount your adventures in Perranporth.

The first line can rhyme with the second,
Describe a person of whom you are fond
Then the third will rhyme with the fourth
With winter storm and wind from the north.

Tell of what, or who arouses passion?
The topics are endless, your choice,
It's not that hard, take my word
Poems must scan with a rhythmic and gentle voice.

*If you can't get the first line to rhyme with the next*
*It really is of no consequence, don't get perplexed.*
*Think of a word which will be easy to rhyme,*
*Say words out loud, plenty of time.*

*Deep inside your soul, deep inside your mind*
*There are feelings to be written, only you can find.*
*Drift on a plateau of solitude and calm,*
*Close your eyes, let emotions form.*

*These words are such a special part of you*
*They tell of times long past, or dreams,*
*They tell of lost love, or love alive and new,*
*They tell of nature, animals and breath-taking extremes.*

*Your words are like a painting*
*They describe a certain scene,*
*The colours fuse, stand proud, take shape*
*Enhanced, a portrait and quite serene.*

*Immerse yourself in a cocktail of words,*
*Dig deep, new colours of expression found*
*Ebb, flow, then on a crescendo float,*
*Be empowered by their meaning and sound.*

*The words and feelings you express*
*Will bubble up straight from your heart*
*So, pluck at them, gather and save*
*Or lose them, as you forget and they depart*

22/2/21

# Have Strength

There will be times when it's dark
And you feel left all alone,
There will be times when it's dark
When you think 'Where's my life gone?'
There will be times when it's dark
And all seems so unfair,
There will be times when it's dark
When the one you love is not there.

There are times when the dawn
Gives hope, expectantly.
There are times when the dawn
Lets you leave despondency,
There are times when the dawn
Gives you an empty stage,
There are times when the dawn
Let's you turn another page.

*There will be times when the light*
*Shows you, you must move on.*
*There will be times when the light*
*Tells you, don't dwell on what has gone.*
*There will be times when the light*
*Shows you opportunities await.*
*There will be times when the light*
*Tells you, step forward, it's not too late.*

*And in the warmth of the sun*
*You know what must be done,*
*And in the warmth of the sun*
*You know a new chapter has begun,*
*And in the warmth of the sun*
*You know you have the strength, so try*
*And in the warmth of the sun*
*You know, your limit is the sky.*

18/3/21

# Jack

The puppy that I wanted,
had been promised to another
So, I chose a tri coloured,
his slightly bigger brother.

I popped back for a second look,
how could I have been in doubt?
Big bundles of fun, with squeaky bark,
playing games and tumbling about.

The day soon came when he could leave
and start his life with me,
But then a phone call with bad news,
trodden on by horse, broken foot and knee.

The lady was quite upset,
what would I like to do?
I knew not to buy an injured puppy,
so politely said, goodbye and thank you.

I searched the local papers
And found what I was looking for,
8 weeks old, both parents here,
I had a choice of four.

I phoned and asked more questions
The answers as I needed to hear,
I set off the following day
To their farm, with directions clear.

I arrived and went into the barn,
There surrounded by bright yellow straw
Fast asleep, after a meal
Were a tangle of tummies, ears and a paw.

The farmer spoke, the puppies woke up,
Happy, healthy, inquisitive and alert,
He whistled, two collies appeared,
Obedient and keen, his parents Bella and Bert.

I picked one up, it was instant love!
He licked my face, lay his head on my shoulder,
His tiny tail wagged around and round,
He snuggled up trying to get closer.

*I couldn't have the first one that I'd seen,*
*So, I put him back on the ground,*
*And picked up his sister; she was sweet*
*But not the character first found.*

*He was biting at my boot with his puppy teeth,*
*And pulling the hem of my jeans,*
*Desperate to climb onto my lap,*
*He'd chosen me it seems!*

*His other two brothers were appealing and well-marked,*
*But this first chap wouldn't leave me alone*
*He climbed up my leg, settled into my lap*
*The farmer smiled and I said, "This is the one."*

*So, money and paperwork changed hands,*
*I'd already decided on a name,*
*This little black and white bundle of love,*
*One syllable 'Jack' he became.*

*He was quick to learn, with a stubborn streak,*
*Wherever I am, so is he,*
*He loves his ball, his walks, his cuddles*
*And monthly trips to the sea.*

*He barks at the waves and runs like the wind,*
*He chases the seagulls when told,*
*He paddles but keeps his paws on the ground,*
*He is so happy, a joy to behold.*

*Well, his love has grown one thousand-fold,*
*He's quick and willing and clever,*
*I've never owned a dog so besotted,*
*And I'll love him deeply, for ever and ever.*

*18/3/21*

*He obviously was meant just for me,*
*He's ten and shows no signs of slowing,*
*He's such a special, special friend*
*And our love continues growing.*

# Sad Ending and New Beginnings

I stood in the lane; we chatted,
"Oh well, I'd better go."
He said, slowly accelerating
In his estate Volvo.

He felt a bump, the car rose up,
The back wheel did the same,
Such a tragic moment
He wasn't to blame.

I looked at the ground, saw her lying there,
Pain and bewilderment in her eyes,
"Oh God, what have I done?"
I heard my neighbour's cries.

She was alive, but couldn't move
Gently we put her into my car

*I drove straight to the vets,*
*Luckily it wasn't far.*

*We carried her into the surgery*
*She couldn't stand unaided,*
*I knew then it was the end*
*Any chance she'd survive faded.*

*They took X-rays, the news was bleak,*
*Her pelvis smashed in many places,*
*There was only one thing I could do*
*A decision many a pet owner faces.*

*Sadly, we said goodbye to Magic*
*And as she peacefully passed away*
*With tears in my eyes and heavy heart*
*She would have been 15 the next day.*

*We waited for a little while,*
*Jack needed a new friend,*
*The house seemed very empty,*
*Such a sad, unhappy end.*

*We made an appointment to visit*
*A rescue centre in Surrey*

We'd been visited, questioned and vetted
The man said, "Perfect home, don't worry."

We took Jack with us
They had to get on and be friends,
But losing Magic still painful
No new dog would make amends.

We waited in a huge enclosure,
They bought dogs in 'one by one',
There were black ones and black and tan,
And a white one, they played, Jack had fun.

She seemed quite sweet, "What do you think,
Shall we have her?" I asked Del.
She was the right age at 18 months,
And they got on really well.

Her first owners lived near Nottingham,
Her second lived in Surrey.
They said her name was Lulu,
We would be owners' number three!

They said she didn't like other dogs,
But mentioned in a casual way,

Carol Anne Skipper

*We didn't realise what that entailed*
*As we watched Jack and Lulu play.*

*Then a few days later,*
*For no reason at all,*
*With ferocious snarl and teeth barred*
*She flew at Jack with intent to maul.*

*Poor Jack, tried to defend himself,*
*Frightened and yelping with pain,*
*Blood splattered from somewhere*
*And on Jack's white bib, a dark stain.*

*No serious damage to either dog,*
*But now we knew why the doner*
*Had given her up for rescue*
*And why we were her third owner.*

*She attacked him twice more,*
*Far heavier and stronger than Jack*
*We had to make a decision*
*Do we admit defeat, take her back?*

*It is never easy with a rescue dog,*
*You make a commitment, so persevere*

*She had had absolutely no training,*
*That was crystal clear.*

*She was quick to learn, easy to train,*
*Her aggressive behaviour towards Jack, now a memory*
*The cleverest GSD we have ever had*
*And a much loved member of our family.*

*If other dogs come into view*
*She has to go on the lead,*
*So, we walk in isolated and remote country*
*Give her as much freedom as she'll need.*

*She loves swimming and fetching balls*
*And enjoys a cup of tea.*
*Was she worth all the hard work?*
*Would I do it again? YES DEFINITELY!*

March 2021

# Depression Explained?

*Depression is always there,*
*It is with you every day*
*It may fade, then surges inwards*
*But it never goes away.*

*Each day you wake, you think, "I'll get through this"*
*Your morning routine ensues*
*The mind is blank, automatic pilot on*
*Whilst what to wear you choose.*

*Your inside feels so empty*
*Your head a fuzzy mess,*
*Language is becoming difficult*
*You say NO when you mean YES.*

*You really can't be bothered,*
*A little sleep will do,*
*It helps to pass the time*
*Till TV switched on to view.*

*You had good reason to be depressed*
*And then P.T.S.D*
*And each hour is a hurdle*
*And each day an infinity.*

*Sometimes you feel OK,*
*Then the black whirlpool drags you down*
*Unable to escape, you fight*
*Nothing to hold onto, you drown.*

*One day the weight is lifted*
*Things don't seem so bad*
*On the surface all is well*
*Except for a small portion of sad.*

*Drugs help a bit*
*They soften the blow*
*But this depression*
*Will just not let go.*

*Today is sunny and warm*
*I'm doing Pilates on Zoom*
*Then out to lunch with girlfriends*
*So why am I full of gloom?*

*I'll chat and laugh and eat and drink*
*But this persona is not me,*
*I'm floating overhead, looking down*
*At the Carol that used to be.*

*Well just got back from The Fox and Hounds*
*4 friends, plus me, met for lunch*
*And after two glasses of wine, fish pie and apricot crumble*
*I realise my friends are such an indispensable bunch.*

*We talked, we laughed, we shared secrets*
*And in confidence told of sadness and dreams,*
*We questioned our existence,*
*Perhaps life not as bleak as it seems.*

*But now at home and on my own*
*The black whirlpool starts to spin*
*The numbness and pain and darkness*
*Rears its ugly head again.*

*4/5/21*

When you suffer from depression you get so good at hiding your sadness. You feel hollow and empty but exude a false happiness to disguise the pain you have inside.

# We Will Always Be Two

I stand in the garden,
Nothing exists, except what I can see,
I am all alone
It was us, now just me.

A feeling of loneliness, of disbelief,
A cold embrace of the unknown
Time stands still, breath shallow
On the brink of nothing, I am drawn down.

My mind is totally empty,
My body numb,
No hunger, no thirst
No tears, but they will come.

Daffodils bow their heads,
Cold wind blows through,
It was us together,
Now it's only you.

Carol Anne Skipper

*You talk to me each day*
*With love or anguished screams*
*Yet I am always by your side*
*And I hold you in your dreams.*

*I wrap you in my love*
*As I am in your heart*
*Not even my departure*
*Can tear our love apart.*

*You will never be alone,*
*I'll watch and care for you,*
*I am never far away,*
*We will always be two.*

10/4/21

HRH The Duke of Edinburgh died 9/4/21.

This poem is for all who have lost someone they truly deeply loved.

# How To Give Up Drinking

I thought I'd cut down on drinking,
Daily intake limit, two glasses of wine
But I just love the taste and when offered
Find it difficult to decline.
I watch the news at 6 on BBC
It's a habit, my daily treat,
With glass of wine and packet of crisps
On settee, day is done, resting feet.

So, I gave myself a firm talking to,
It's not doing you any good,
Also, it makes you hungry
And you end up eating junk food.
What else could I drink at night?
I don't like fizzy drinks or fruit juice,
Too much tea stains your teeth brown,
Calories I need to reduce.

I wander around the shop
Inspiration is what I need
Still water I can get from a tap
Must enjoy the taste if I am to succeed.
Non-alcoholic lager is too fizzy
Makes your tummy bloated,
Fruit cordial full of saccharine
Your tongue with white is coated.

Then hidden in a darkest corner
Non-alcoholic wine I see,
There is red and white and rosé,
So, I gather up all three.
That night at 6 with crisps in bowl
And feet on stool I watch the news,
I try the white, it's very good
So similar to real wine, easy to confuse.

I down that glass, I'm most impressed
Tastes just like the real thing
And at only £2.75 a bottle…
Then a warning bell begins to ring,
I finish off the second glass
And much to my dismay
Upon checking the bottle
It's my favourite Chardonnay!

14/5/21

# Second Covid Vaccination

Well, it's 10am, it's Friday, and here I am again,
Deep in the jungle of Crawley, I can already feel the pain.
I'm being very brave, the weeks in-between just flew
Alone I approach the door, Jenny not in view.

A ream of questions, now checked in,
I'm trapped, no escape, sit and wait,
Shrouded in green uniform and approaching fast,
Cath leads me to my fate.

I'm in the cubicle, we sit and chat,
I warm to her, she's kind,
"I'm not doing it till you relax your arm;" she said,
So I did, all over and vaccination card signed.

Next into the final seated area,
with two firemen I had to wait,
Tight black T-shirts, large chests,
Arms strong, they greatly increased my heart rate!

Carol Anne Skipper

*So back at home no side effects,*
*Slight ache in my left arm,*
*I've had both vaccinations,*
*Soon I'll be immune and cannot come to harm.*

*11/5/21*

# My Husband

He doesn't ever notice
If I buy a brand new dress.
He doesn't ever notice
If the house is in a mess.
He doesn't ever notice
If I buy myself some flowers.
He doesn't ever notice
If I don't talk to him for hours.
He doesn't ever notice
If a pretty top, I buy.
He doesn't ever notice
If I'm happy or if I cry.
He doesn't ever notice
If I'm fat or if I'm thin.
He doesn't ever notice
If I'm out more than I'm in.
He doesn't ever notice
If the garden is full of weeds.

Carol Anne Skipper

*He didn't even notice*
*When I filled his shoe with centipedes.*
*He doesn't ever notice*
*When my hair is a different shade,*
*I don't think he'd notice*
*if men from Mars invade.*
*He doesn't ever notice*
*When the dogs have not been fed.*
*Do you think he'll notice*
*When this hammer hits his head?*
*(More than once?)*

*17/5/21*

# Things Aren't What They Used To Be

*In your head you are still twenty,*
*But unfortunately you are…not,*
*You need to spend the day gardening*
*Prune the hedge, grass grown a lot.*
*Pull up weeds, dead head rose,*
*Re-pot flowers, strim the edge,*
*The hanging baskets need water*
*Check that nest, babies ready to fledge.*

*But after just an hour or so*
*Your body begins to complain,*
*Your back is stooped and ridged*
*Your knees seize up in pain,*
*Your hands have pins and needles*
*And for breath you fight,*
*Husband said we need a gardener*
*And for once I think he's right….*

7/6/21

# The Holiday

Well, the first day of our holiday didn't go too well
In fact, as I shall recount, it was the day from hell!

The lady in the right-hand lane
was waving frantically,
So, I waved back and said to Del
"Who the bloody hell is she?"

At the same moment he said, "Oh no,
We've a puncture in the caravan,"
I said "Do not worry,
We'll phone the AA man."

So, we limped onto the service road,
The tyre completely shredded,
The alloy wheel was flat not round
And in the road embedded.

Carol Anne Skipper

*"It's not a problem," I said casually*
*As I phoned the AA man*
*And sure enough, within ½ an hour*
*There he was, in his bright yellow van.*

*By now the rain was heavy,*
*I stayed in the car warm and dry,*
*I ate Mint Imperials, did puzzles*
*Had a snooze, the time, it just flew by!*

*Finally, spare wheel and tyre in place*
*And we continued on our way*
*Through high winds and rain to the campsite,*
*Is this really the middle of May?*

*The rain eased off but not the wind,*
*Next job, erect the awning,*
*That was where the dogs would sleep,*
*No, we couldn't leave it till morning.*

*First Del put pole into canvas*
*And I hung on tight to one corner*
*Elements against us and we finally won,*
*(Someone had left the food behind!)*
*But with nothing to eat for dinner!*

*Dogs fed, Del to shop*
*Purchased drink and food*
*What an awful, long, long day*
*Will tomorrow bring better mood?*

*Saturday*

*Visit Tyneham village*
*Evacuated suddenly (and permanently)*
*Enter Church and Schoolhouse*
*Understand, absorb their history.*

*Walk along to Kimmeridge Bay*
*Rain stopped luckily,*
*Past army firing range*
*"Keep Out" signs state menacingly.*

*Arrive at cliff top*
*Wind blows ferociously*
*Gaze at boiling sea below*
*2 canoeists acting irresponsibly.*

*Sunday*

*Enjoyable drive to Swanage*
*Tide incoming swiftly,*

*Dogs run along remaining sand*
*Barking excitedly.*

*Now snuggled up in caravan*
*Rain beats down relentlessly.*
*Pizzas warm in oven,*
*White wine sipped delicately.*

*Monday*

*Off to Ringstead beach*
*£6.00 to park, daylight robbery*
*Yet isolated and remote*
*So paid reluctantly.*

*Walked on pebbles, wind in our faces*
*Del sat down exhaustedly*
*I explored beach, dogs swam*
*Sun came out unexpectedly.*

*Then sudden squall*
*Rain pours down violently*
*Quick march towards café*
*Hot tea drunk gratefully.*

### Tuesday

*Trees on hilltop bent and twisted*
*By winds blown ferociously,*
*Dry stone walls nestle into*
*The Purbeck Hills moulded delicately.*

*Studland Bay, 4 miles of golden sand*
*Blue sky and sun warm, most unusually,*
*Calm sea pushes ripples to shore,*
*Yacht with 2 red sails flap noisily.*

*Our warm day became windy and cold,*
*Back to caravan, raining persistently*
*Wine in glass, table laid,*
*Fish and Chip van arriving shortly.*

### Wednesday

*Perched high, visible to all at sea*
*Portland Bill lighthouse, painted recently,*
*Bright white at top and bottom*
*And coloured blood red centrally.*

*Magnificent Chesil Beach*
*A scrunch of stones curve gently*

*Disappear toward a distant haze*
*Leading eye to infinity.*

*Thursday*

*Ferry across to Sandbanks,*
*Sun's rays tan face beautifully,*
*Sit on open top bus and explore,*
*Then to beach, warm sand caress feet erotically.*

*Friday*

*Gaze up at Corfe Castle*
*One single wall perpendicular and mighty,*
*Other walls, tumbled down, lie forgotten and forlorn*
*Stone arches, off centre, balance precariously.*

*Yet the ruins hold such power*
*Over a thousand years of history*
*Ghostly whispers of Servants, Squires and Kings*
*William the 1st, to Elizabeth finally.*

*Last year peregrine falcons nested*
*Will they return annually?*
*Explore narrow winding lanes*
*Stone cottages snuggle intimately.*

*Tea and homemade scones*
*In cottage garden, devoured greedily,*
*Then Durlston Country Park (overlooking sea)*
*Dolphins and seals appear frequently (but not when we went.)*

*Saturday*

*We are on a number 50 bus*
*Open top, lurches and sways scarily,*
*To explore Swanage shops and sea,*
*Overhead branches low, beware, hit occasionally.*

*Walk along seafront and coastal path,*
*Sun hot, so, dressed scantily,*
*Dogs enjoy cooling paddle and swim,*
*Quick shop, return on bus, wind blows coldly.*

*Sunday*

*Dogs for final walk*
*Enjoy the panoramic view,*
*If the M25 isn't gridlocked*
*Then we'll be home by two.*

Carol Anne Skipper

*But we didn't go on the motorway*
*He took the scenic route,*
*Luckily, we had some food*
*And water stored in the boot.*

*Because Petworth was closed*
*And the diversion signs we did follow*
*It's beginning to get dark now*
*Perhaps we'll get home by tomorrow…*

May 2021

100

# Relapse

You don't want to get out of bed,
You don't want to lift your head,
You just want to stare at the wall,
You just want to forget it all.

You hope it will go away
With the start of each new day,
But you are stuck in the mud of gloom
When will normal life resume?

Some days seem better than before
But most days are worse, 'sods law'
Pull yourself together and get on with life,
Why is there always a pain? Cuts sharp like a knife.

One day the pain seems less
The future you must address
You can smile, life is ok,
And tomorrow starts today.

26/6/21

# It's A Mystery

I plumped up the pillows
The duvet I shook
Bottom sheet straightened
Bed neat and tidy, good look

"What on earth are you doing,"
With straight face, he said,
"Have you really no idea?" I replied,
"It's called Making The Bed."

August 2021

# My Friend Jack (Again!)

The greeting I get every morning
Is one that lifts my heart,
Black ears pricked and happy grin
But overnight we've been apart.

He sits beside me, snuggles close,
I tell him what the day will bring
And he holds his head to one side
He understands everything.

I go outside, animals to feed
He's behind me all the way
He knows that very shortly
He and I will play

"Shall we have a game? shall we?"
I say to his delight
And off he goes to collect his ball
From where it was left last night.

*I throw the ball and it's returned*
*He never runs out of puff,*
*But I've got other things to do,*
*"Jack" I tell him "That's enough."*

*Head tilted left; pink tongue exposed*
*He's as happy as can be*
*He knows that now it is breakfast time*
*Which is eaten hungrily.*

*Jack Takes Over*

*Oh, look she's doing gardening*
*I'll help, I always do.*
*I dig some holes and pick up sticks,*
*Then I roll in badger poo!*

*I don't think she is very pleased with me,*
*She's gone indoors to get*
*Some warm and soapy water*
*And now my side is wet!*

*I see her put her wellies on*
*And in her pocket my silver whistle*

*She should know by now that's a waste of time,*
*I've selective hearing and the speed of a missile.*

*So off we go around the fields,*
*I paddle and drink in the streams*
*I chase a rabbit, yes it escapes*
*I'll have to run faster it seems!*

*And now the day is ended,*
*I'm warm, I'm tired, I'm fed,*
*I've had my goodnight treat,*
*I think I'll go to bed.*

*I rest my head upon my paws*
*And snuggle down into cushions deep,*
*My eyes close, my breathing slows,*
*I drift off…now fast asleep…*

September 2021

# Hypocrites Both

They bought a farm in the country
She said it was his dream,
But all the time he was planning,
He had a money-making scheme.

He didn't do much farming,
He cut down trees instead,
He shot deer, butchered where they fell
Once green, grass stained bright red!

But he tried to be so friendly,
Two-faced and a hypocrite,
He never seemed quite at ease,
Creepy, couldn't quite put my finger on it.

She seemed so sweet and gentle,
A friend I thought I had
But her intentions were evil,
Just like him, two-faced and bad.

Carol Anne Skipper

*They were not country people,*
*They didn't have a clue,*
*The farm buildings fell into disrepair*
*The rotten fencing lying in full view.*

*The ditches never cleaned out*
*Speed bumps put in the wrong place,*
*He took no advice; he knew it all*
*The internet his knowledge base.*

*They pretended to love nature,*
*'Count the dragonflies by the lake'*
*Bat boxes put up in trees*
*Wildflower meadows, all so fake.*

*They had only one intention*
*As scum with no morals do,*
*Destroy a rural idyll, make money*
*Then move to pastures new.*

*Leaving neighbours lives in tatters,*
*House prices less than half,*
*Lorries, vans, cars, roar past*
*Now storage, distribution, offices and staff.*

*Annihilate all farmland*
*You don't give a toss*
*No longer a green and pleasant land*
*Just needed to acquire a tax loss.*

*He built a road down to his lake*
*Then men would pay to go and fish,*
*But the only thing to be caught*
*Leptospirosis, another illogical wish.*

*"It ain't gonna happen," he said to me,*
*With an arrogant sneer and a laugh,*
*As I suggested the logical place*
*To re-route the adjacent footpath.*

*Did he think that language was clever?*
*Did his bully boy tactics make him feel big?*
*I just thought he was common*
*An insignificant, inarticulate pig.*

*Well, will he obtain the council's consent?*
*Another A.O.N.B bites the dust.*
*They have only one aim, to make money*
*They fill me with total disgust!*

Carol Anne Skipper

*I've cried so many tears*
*Since the council's letter came through*
*And no matter what the decision*
*I want nothing, nothing ever to do with either of you!!*

November 2022

# My Birthday

I've requested no presents on the day,
And the reason will become clear,
I'd like fun, laughter and memories,
To last throughout the year.

It took me a while to write this poem,
There are so many things I'd like to do,
But I'm only one half of this adventure,
The other half is you!

So please take me somewhere
I've never been before
Offer me new experiences
And let my spirits soar.

Or take me somewhere I know and love,
I'll share my memories with you,
Surround me in beauty and solitude
Stone walls, sweeping hills, endless view.

*Is a helicopter flight over Manhattan*
*A bit too much to ask?*
*OK I'll settle for a whisky tasting*
*Straight from an old oak cask.*

*Plan a trip to Eastbourne*
*See a tribute band near the pier,*
*Stay overnight, eat fish and chips*
*Drink Cava, what a lovely idea!*

*Walk along a beach with me*
*Hard sand beneath our feet*
*Sun overhead, a cloudless sky*
*The tide in calm retreat.*

*A pair of size 4 Jimmy Choo's*
*Is what I'd really like,*
*But if I'm being too optimistic*
*We could hire an electric bike.*

*Take me to a concert*
*The ballet or a play*
*A musical in London*
*We could watch the matinée*

A stately home or gardens
T' would be enjoyable for me
National Trust, English Heritage
Being a member, I get in free.

Lunch at a beamed country pub,
The Observatory at Herstmonceaux,
Or Petworth, Batemans, Numans
Or Wakehurst; where shall we go?

Take me on a steam train
Or The Orient Express
10 days on an African Safari
Would be pushing my luck, I guess.

Let's go fishing off the rocks
In a beautiful Cornish bay
Or visit the Isles of Scilly
For a long weekend, what do you say?

We could go paddleboarding
Upon the calm blue sea,
Or indulge in a naughty
Calorie laden afternoon tea.

*I've never done a murder mystery*
*An escape room would be fun*
*We could stay overnight in a hotel*
*I'm sure it could be done.*

*Perhaps a day at the races*
*Or a local County Show*
*Just happy to spend time in the fresh air*
*With people I love and know.*

*We must grab the moment whilst it's here*
*And enjoy doing things together*
*Let's get up and do it now*
*Lest we lose the chance forever.*

December 2020

*PS:*
*I've got enough jewellery, clothes*
*Shoes, gadgets and whatever,*
*So, let's have fun just you and me*
*And spend some time together.*
*xx*

I was 70 in January 2022; I wanted a year to remember.
So far I have not been disappointed.

# The Scruffy Side of Vagrant

My husband is on the scruffy side of vagrant
He's worn the same clothes for years
He has lots of new and fashionable gear
but the old ones are what he prefers.
Today he's wearing camouflage trousers
Two shades of green and brown,
Around his ankles string pulled tight
Leather belt stops them falling down.

Stretched across his manly chest
Red T-shirt with splashes of paint
With grey fishing hat upon his head
An attractive look it ain't.
Upon his feet grey plimsolls
Bought in '72
When he walks the soles flap open
"But" he says," The laces are new."

And to complete this amazing ensemble
A multi-coloured cardigan, with broken zip at the front,
Elbows long since worn away
Not a pleasant sight, to be perfectly blunt.
So should the weather become inclement
And should the sun refuse to shine
He'll wear his pièce de résistance,
Which is the least favourite of mine!

An old green waterproof coat
All pockets filled with 'stuff',
With big hole under left armpit
And the lining hanging off.
He could make a tramp look stylish
But he just doesn't care one jot,
One day I'll fill black bin bags
And throw away the lot.

11/6/21

# Lost And Found

Grey mists swirled
Problems abound
How could she escape
Be free from the ground

Waiting and wondering
When would she go?
Was God against her
How could she know?

Suddenly a light came
A chance to break free
Wind carried her upward
Wings beat rhythmically.

Then far below her
Surrounded by sea
An island so perfect
Serene in beauty

*She swooped and landed*
*Air pure and clear*
*Had she found her idyll?*
*Had she found it here?*

*Food in abundance*
*A warmth and a love*
*A caring hand*
*A glimpse of heaven above.*

*Gentleness, tenderness,*
*Laughter and sun*
*Forget your worries,*
*They never began.*

*One day it happened*
*The grey mists closed in*
*Cold clutched at her heart*
*Oh, what was her sin?*

*Tears flowed downwards*
*She tried to suppress,*
*Brown eyes widened*
*Lest others guess.*

*I don't wish to go now*
*Please don't make me leave*
*But coldness abounded*
*No sign of reprieve.*

*Grey mists engulfed her*
*Rain began to fall*
*Had she been dreaming*
*And not escaped at all?*

July 1996

Sometimes life is not kind, then an invitation came to visit one of the smaller, less populated Channel Islands, but holidays do not last forever....

121

# *Unrequited Love*

*I spoke the words best left unsaid*
*But you knew and you cut me dead,*
*You gently said, "It's not to be,"*
*There's no spark, no electricity.*
*You wouldn't use me, you couldn't lie,*
*Rejected and lonely you made me cry.*

*I need someone to hold me close*
*And hug me when I'm down.*
*I need someone to say I'm here*
*Just phone and I'll be round.*
*I need someone who makes me laugh*
*To be strong when I am weak.*
*I need someone to talk to*
*Help me turn the other cheek.*
*I need someone to help me up*
*When self-esteem is low.*
*I need someone in the dark of night*
*To whisper, "Please don't go."*

*I need someone to lie with*
*And give my body to.*
*I need someone to kiss me*
*I dreamed it would be you.*

*So now I know the way ahead*
*And our friendship will remain*
*We will still meet and laugh together*
*And I'll try and hide my pain.*

July 1996

# Round Two

*Ok so here we go again,*
*Council's letter arrived today,*
*They have reapplied for planning permission*
*They think no one should stand in their way!*

*Another pair of millionaires*
*Who make money by fair means or foul,*
*But you are up against a feisty bunch,*
*Not giving in, we fight cheek by jowl.*

*We won't allow you to desecrate*
*The area in which we live,*
*The beauty which surrounds us all*
*Gives stamina, not one inch will we give!!*

*Why buy a farm in such an isolated place*
*And then wish to spoil it forever*
*Your neighbours will stand firm and strong*
*Against you, united, whatever!*

Carol Anne Skipper

*Once again, let battle commence,*
*Objections sent, so pariahs take heed,*
*Now anger and hate hang low in the air,*
*Time you moved, cut your losses, concede.*

1/4/22

# Bill Roberts

*Bill Roberts is a hoarder,*
*There's nothing he won't keep,*
*Near the front gate planks of wood*
*And under tarpaulin a second heap.*

*The woodshed has logs for burning,*
*But more wood at the side is stored.*
*"Do you know the price of wood?*
*Throw it away, don't be absurd."*

*In the three-bay open barn*
*A caravanette and 101,*
*The car not moved since '93*
*And the lorry's brakes have gone.*

*And piled between these two old heaps,*
*Yet more wood is lying there,*
*On top of that garden furniture*
*Three wooden benches and a chair.*

*In front of this rests a five-bar gate*
*Concrete mixer and bags of coal,*
*A generator and fencing posts*
*Old gear box and scaffolding pole.*

*Note the white Freelander van*
*Parked across the 'new barn' door*
*A deterrent should the thieves return*
*Who broke in a few months before.*

*They smashed the locks and entered the barn*
*With intent to steal what they could carry,*
*But when they saw such quantity of stuff*
*They realised they needed a lorry!*

*The sight that met their greedy eyes,*
*Piled so high that none could get past*
*I will recount in the next few verses,*
*Nothing taken, they couldn't be arsed.*

*Bang in the middle a white Range Rover*
*'V' reg, 2 doors, quite old.*
*"That will be worth a lot of money*
*Once done up and when it is sold."*

*A large pine Welsh Dresser,*
*Far too big for the kitchen he's got,*
*It was free to collector and not far away,*
*He read the advert and was off like a shot!*

*At the back of the barn, wooden shelves bend*
*With the weight of jars and a blue biscuit tin,*
*There is nothing in any of them*
*But they will be handy, for putting things in.*

*A roof box for a car, not sure of the make,*
*Is dusty and lain at the top*
*Of batteries, roof tiles and pallets*
*Paint tins, creosote and old fashioned mop.*

*There are piles of tyres, an old wardrobe*
*Filled with fishing line, rods and catch net.*
*Next to chain saws, strimmer's and tow ropes,*
*Are mowers, petrol cans and croquet set.*

*Old broken hoovers – great for spares*
*Lie alongside furniture, once owned by his mum,*
*"I'll paint them, it's Shabby Chic*
*And it will sell for a tidy sum."*

*The problem is he acquires all this stuff*
*Nothing is ever thrown away,*
*And the answer that he always gives?*
*"It will come in handy one day!!!"*

March 2022

130

# The Tail End

*From Jack and Lulu…*

*They took us to Swanage,*
*We swam in the sea,*
*We sniffed and explored,*
*We've just had our tea*
*Paws are tired, body still wet,*
*Now fast asleep, don't wake us just yet.*

# *Advanced Bookings Only*

*Advanced bookings only*
*Said the sign on the taxi door.*
*I've I booked one for tomorrow*
*Not yesterday or the day before.*

# Jack's Tick

*I found a tick on Jack's side*
*Bulbus body, legs wriggle and writhe*
*Well, I smothered it with neat vodka,*
*You're right it didn't survive!*

Lightning Source UK Ltd.
Milton Keynes UK
UKHW020810091022
410146UK00007B/43